Volume 4

The Industrial Revolution Comes to America

James R. Arnold & Roberta Wiener

Grolier

An imprint of Scholastic Library Publishing
Danbury, Connecticut

First published in 2005 by Grolier
An imprint of Scholastic Library Publishing
Old Sherman Turnpike
Danbury, Connecticut 06816

For information address the publisher:
Scholastic Library Publishing, Old Sherman Turnpike,
Danbury, Connecticut 06816

Library of Congress Cataloging-in-Publication Data

Arnold, James R.
    The industrial revolution / James R. Arnold and Roberta Wiener.
    p. cm
    Includes bibliographical references and index.
    Contents: v. 1. A turning point in history – v. 2. The industrial revolution begins – v. 3. The industrial revolution spreads – v. 4. The industrial revolution comes to America – v. 5. The growth of the industrial revolution in America – v. 6. The industrial revolution spreads through Europe – v. 7. The worldwide industrial revolution – v. 8. America's second industrial revolution – v. 9. The industrial revolution and the working class v. 10. The industrial revolution and American society.
    ISBN 0-7172-6031-3 (set)—ISBN 0-7172-6032-1 (v. 1)—
ISBN 0-7172-6033-X (v. 2)—ISBN 0-7172-6034-8 (v. 3)—
ISBN 0-7172-6035-6 (v. 4)—ISBN 0-7172-6036-4 (v. 5)—
ISBN 0-7172-6037-2 (v. 6)—ISBN 0-7172-6038-0 (v. 7)—
ISBN 0-7172-6039-9 (v. 8)—ISBN 0-7172-6040-2 (v. 9)—
ISBN 0-7172-6041-0 (v. 10)
    1. Industrial revolution. 2. Economic history. I. Wiener, Roberta.
II. Title.

HD2321.A73 2005
330.9'034–dc22

2004054243

Printed and bound in China

CONTENTS

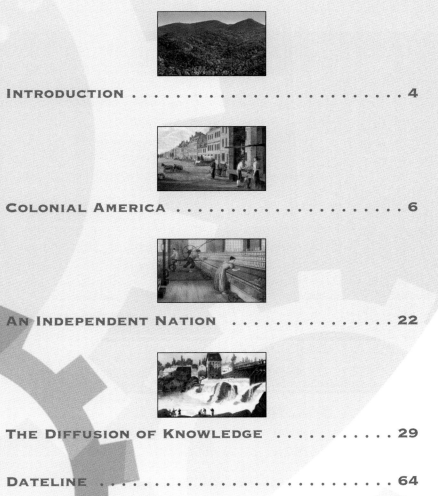

INTRODUCTION

The United States enjoyed a set of advantages that enabled it to industrialize at a rate second only to Great Britain. Many of the advantages derived from the fact that the nation grew from English roots.

Just as in England, America had a set of successful merchant capitalists who believed economic growth was good for the nation. They had a particular interest in promoting industry and agriculture because they benefitted personally. They were an aggressive, self-confident group who were always looking for new opportunities to make money. The European elite, however, were born into the aristocratic class. They looked down on people who spent their lives pursuing money, viewing them as "mere merchants."

The United States was more egalitarian. Unlike the British, Americans did not have kings and queens nor a wealthy, land-owning aristocracy. More so than even English society, American culture gave social status to those who possessed wealth. People who were economically successful rose to the top of American society.

The United States also enjoyed some unique natural advantages. When the first European settlers arrived, they found

Nearly impenetrable forests covered most of the eastern United States. In America the forests were both obstacle and resource. Trees had to be cleared from the land to create farmland, roads, and homesteads. They also provided the main building material for houses, a valuable commodity for export, and fuel for the fires of industry.

tremendous hardwood forests. The trees grew so densely that people said a squirrel could travel from the Atlantic coastline to the Mississippi River without having to touch the ground. While England and some areas of western Europe were running out of trees, America possessed abundant timber for construction and for **charcoal** manufacture. Also, compared to Europe, more regions had access to flowing water that could provide power to turn **mills**.

In Europe guilds made up of skilled craftsmen zealously defended their privileges and blocked modernization. However, Europeans did not bring the guild structure with them to the new land.

The Industrial Revolution depended on a growing population to provide both workers and consumers. Important factors that contributed to rapid population growth in Europe included improved diet for the poorer classes, better public sanitation that reduced the spread of waterborne diseases, and the development of the smallpox vaccine, which reduced deaths from epidemic disease.

The United States shared in all of those developments but, compared to Europe, also had higher birthrates and lower death rates. Furthermore, more than six million immigrants arrived at America's ports between 1800 and 1870, and another 25 million arrived during the subsequent 50 years. As a result, during the nineteenth century the American population boomed.

Another unique American characteristic shaped the country's early industrial experience. From colonial times through the first decades of the nation's existence land was cheap. Americans preferred to work their own land rather than work for someone else. That made hired labor scarce and expensive. The scarcity and high cost of labor provided an incentive to invent and use labor-saving devices, substituting machines for workers in order to increase profits.

Wealthy Americans built fine homes that imitated English homes in style.

CHARCOAL: a fuel made by charring wood in a buried fire so that very little air enters the fire

MILL: building with repetitive, rotary machinery for processing an item such as grain, gunpowder, lumber, metal, or textiles. The earliest mills were water-powered gristmills that used millstones to grind grain into flour.

COLONIAL AMERICA

When the first English colonists came to Virginia and Massachusetts, everything they needed including food had to be imported from England. Later, during the first years on the frontier settlers lived at a bleak subsistence level. They had to clear the dense forests to create open fields for planting and bring their crops to harvest before the start of winter. They

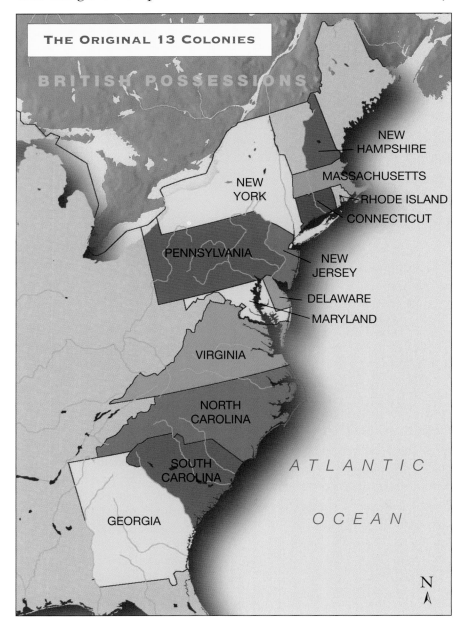

THE ORIGINAL 13 COLONIES

BRITISH POSSESSIONS

NEW HAMPSHIRE
MASSACHUSETTS
NEW YORK
RHODE ISLAND
CONNECTICUT
PENNSYLVANIA
NEW JERSEY
DELAWARE
MARYLAND
VIRGINIA
NORTH CAROLINA
SOUTH CAROLINA
GEORGIA

ATLANTIC OCEAN

N

The first English colony in America failed when 116 men, women, and children disappeared from an island off the coast of North Carolina some time after 1587. From this harrowing beginning the 13 colonies had grown to a population of about 2.5 million by the time they declared their independence from Great Britain in 1776.

had to adjust to new environmental conditions and learn about an unfamiliar, complex mix of climate, soils, crops, and pests. For most of the first European settlers in each of the thirteen colonies life was difficult, and survival hung in the balance. Yet the lure of owning land, something that was not a possibility for members of Europe's lower classes, brought thousands of immigrants to the British colonies each year.

As the decades passed, the frontier moved steadily west. On the frontier the struggle for survival usually mirrored the experiences of the first settlers. But east of the frontier a stable pattern of life became established. The colonists attempted to put in place familiar practices, using the tools and technology they had used at home in Europe. The land they came from was mostly rural, and most Europeans had relied on a combination of farming and home manufacture (cottage industry) to support themselves. So it was in America, where about 80 percent of all colonists grew their own food and earned their livelihood as self-employed agricultural workers.

After they became established, farmers got adequate nutrition, but their typical meals were monotonous and

Colonists in America cut down trees to build their houses, creating clearings and fields in the process.

7

unbalanced. A Swedish traveler described the diet of typical farmers living in New York in the 1750s: "[for breakfast] drank tea ... and with the tea they ate bread and butter and radishes. ...At noon they had a regular meal, meat served with turnips and cabbage. In the evening they made a porridge of corn ... into which they poured fresh milk. ...This was their supper nearly every evening."

Colonial Americans mostly dressed themselves in wool and linen, using these materials to make everything from shirts and trousers to bodices and petticoats. A "homespun" man's coat, made in Virginia during the 1780s out of a blended wool and cotton fabric.

COLONIAL MANUFACTURE

In favorable locations along the Atlantic coast cities developed. But the great majority of colonial Americans lived in rural settings that were poorly served by roads. Consequently, most colonial manufacturers produced goods for the local market. Freight costs were simply too high for them to sell to more distant places. The leading manufacturers included saddlers,

When people familiar with industrial practices in Europe first came to America during the 1700s, they were surprised to see the Americans utilizing old-fashioned techniques and processes. An early American blacksmith at work

hatters, blacksmiths, weavers, boot and shoemakers, and woodworkers. All manufacture was on a small scale

Most settlements during early colonial times suffered from a lack of skilled craftsmen. About one in ten American workers was a skilled artisan such as a blacksmith, tanner, or millwright. During the years leading up to the American Revolution almost all manufacture was for domestic use, including the making of cloth to clothe the family. Cloth-

Spinning was so associated with a woman's work that the expression "the distaff side" (a distaff is a tool used in spinning) is still used to describe the female partner in a marriage.

Home textiles production:
See also
Volume 2 pages 6-10

making was a particularly important household enterprise with specific chores assigned to each sex. To make linen, the family planted flax, which grew exceptionally well in the colonies. Two acres of flax yielded about 300 pounds of plants at harvest. After allowing the harvested plants to rot and dry, the men used a heavy log set in a frame (called a brake) to crush and break apart the plants. This separated the fibers from the woody part of the plants. Women and children then carefully combed the fibers to separate them for spinning. Wool required even more combing, using a hand device called a card.

Using home spinning wheels—an indispensable household tool—women spun the fiber into yarn. It was time-consuming, tedious work. Both men and women wove cloth using hand looms. Wealthier families living in urban settings took their yarn to a professional hand loom weaver. After weaving, women cleaned and finished the cloth and—in the case of wool cloth—pounded, or fulled, it to thicken and compress the cloth.

Opposite: A teenage girl described in her diary spending January and February spinning and March through May weaving to produce enough cloth to meet her family's needs. When she finished on June 1, she wrote: "Welcome sweet Liberty!"

Below left: Early colonial brick manufacture was a primitive process, involving hard labor. Workers dug clay by hand and then put it in forms to dry, first in the air, and then in ovens.

Below right: Americans took pride in economic independence. George Washington wore a suit of homespun cloth at his first inauguration in 1789.

On the eve of the Industrial Revolution the home manufacture of cloth took place in all except the very poorest and very richest households. Farm households in particular devoted much of the time from December to May to spinning and weaving. As was the case in England, the introduction of powered machinery to perform those hand operations helped launch the Industrial Revolution in the United States.

Colonial industry, such as it was, was limited by the availability of natural resources and the difficulties of transportation across a primitive frontier. Early colonists made do with local resources. They fired bricks from locally dug clay, sawed lumber from the surrounding forests, used convenient flowing water to grind grain into flour, mined and smelted iron ore where they found it. Because iron was scarce and expensive while wood was abundant and practically free, whenever possible everything was built out of wood. Transportation barriers meant that most industries were located either near ports or along navigable rivers.

British mercantile policy also worked against the development of large industry. Britain did not want its colonies to manufacture products that would compete with those made in the British Isles. Instead, British leaders viewed their colonies, including those in North America, as sources of raw

Bellows:
See also
Volume 1 page 10

materials for the homeland and as markets for goods manufactured in England. Furthermore, by law the colonies could not import manufactured goods from outside the British Empire. By late colonial times manufactured goods or semimanufactured goods (such as pig iron or indigo that had been partly processed for use in making other products) from England made up nearly 80 percent of total American imports.

In spite of all obstacles, an industrial economy in America slowly emerged. The greatest progress came in the iron industry.

THE COLONIAL IRON INDUSTRY

The first European settlers in North America relied on supplies from Europe to meet their needs for manufactured goods. The supplies were expensive and their arrival in the settlements erratic. Consequently colonists tried to exploit local raw materials to develop their own manufacturing as soon as they could.

English settlers built the first iron works in British North America in 1619 at a location upriver from Jamestown. There settlers tried, without a great deal of success, to forge iron from local deposits of iron ore. Massachusetts colonists had greater success when they tried 25 years later. Soon simple iron works sprang up in favorable locations throughout New England.

A bellows provided a simple way to make a fire burn hotter by blowing air into it. Still, the blacksmith had to pump the bellows by hand.

Cross-section view of a blast furnace. The thick, lined walls withstood the great heat generated by the furnace. Hand-operated bellows were first replaced by water-powered bellows. By the late 1700s waterwheels drove pistons to compress air in cylinders, and the compressed air provided a powerful blast to heat the furnace.

Blast furnaces:
See also
Volume 2 page 35

BLAST FURNACE: a tall furnace that uses a blast of air to generate intense heat capable of melting iron and processing it into a purer form

The earliest colonial iron works were bloomery forges, no different from those used in Medieval Europe. Workers heated iron ore over charcoal fires and used leather bellows to increase the temperature. Then they hammered the mass (called a bloom, it never reached its melting temperature) into shape to produce a crude wrought iron. In effect, the bloomery forge was nothing more than an oversized blacksmith's forge.

Gradually more modern **blast furnace**s replaced the bloomeries. A typical North American blast furnace was a stone pyramid standing 30 or more feet high. Workers fed iron ore, charcoal, and limestone into the furnace and left it to cook for several hours to yield a high-quality molten iron (the temperatures were high enough to melt the iron into a liquid state). Workers skimmed the slag, or waste material, off the liquid and then directed it into trenches (called "sows") dug into the sandy floor. The liquid iron then ran into a series of side trenches (called "pigs," hence the term "pig iron"). Alternatively, the liquid iron could be poured directly into molds to make kettles, bells, or even cannons.

Builders located the blast furnaces in places that combined nearby, shallow iron ore deposits (to avoid the cost and labor of deep mining), abundant hardwood timber for charcoal, and dependable flowing water to power the air blast. Entire villages, called "iron plantations," sprang up in such favorable sites. There forges used large, heavy, water-powered hammers to beat the iron pigs to remove carbon and make wrought iron. Blacksmiths purchased the wrought iron to fabricate such items as horseshoes or spades.

More than any other colony, Pennsylvania had the natural resources to support an iron industry. By 1771 it had more than 50 furnaces and forges, and was the leading iron producer in British America. By 1776 the 13 British colonies produced one-seventh of the world supply of pig and wrought iron.

Great Britain responded to American industrialization by passing laws restricting the emigration of skilled workers from Britain and by forbidding the construction of modern mills and

Europe's population tripled in the hundred years after the Industrial Revolution began. A view of London at the beginning of the Industrial Revolution

manufacturing facilities. For example, in 1750 Parliament passed an Iron Act that limited the American industry to the production of pig and bar iron while forbidding the building of slitting mills (where the iron was heated again and run between rollers to produce plates or rods). Consequently, American manufacturers had to export pig and bar iron to England, where British forges reworked it into finished metal products. The British manufacturers exported the finished work back to the colonies. Not only did Americans have to pay customs duties, but most of the profit from iron manufacture came from the sale of finished goods, and that profit was denied to them. The Iron Act was one of many unfair British trade policies that angered American colonists.

Political tensions between the colonists and England worsened after the end of the French and Indian War in 1763. Leaders of the opposition to British rule argued that the colonists had to become self-sufficient. In 1774 the Massachusetts Committee of Safety made a series of resolutions regarding manufacturing. They urged the people to produce everything from iron nails to steel. The delegates knew that American manufacturing was not keeping up with the innovations taking place in England. They recommended the establishment of learned societies to establish "such arts and manufactures as may be useful to this people and are not yet introduced."

Patriots, as they called themselves, also organized economic **boycotts** of English goods in an effort to change British policies. Thomas Jefferson drafted a resolution for the Virginia House of Burgesses in 1774 that recommended economic boycott until Parliament repealed certain laws, including "the acts prohibiting or restraining internal manufactures in America." At that time the Industrial Revolution was well under way in England, but the colonies remained in a preindustrial

Above: In addition to his medical practice Dr. Benjamin Rush helped establish the United Company of Philadelphia for Promoting Manufactures in 1775. One of its goals was to manufacture cloth and end reliance on British textiles. The company somehow acquired a design for a spinning jenny and opened a factory.

BOYCOTT: an agreement to refuse to buy from or sell to certain businesses

Left: Benjamin Franklin argued in favor of American self-sufficiency: "I do not know a single imported article into the northern colonies, but what they can either do without or make themselves."

COLONIAL INDUSTRY

Below: A pair of leather shoes made by hand in Colonial America. In 1760 Samuel Lane, a New Hampshire farmer and shoemaker wrote "This week past my 2 sons Sam in the 14th and Joshua in the 12th year of their ages made 14 pair of women's pumps."

Bottom: Colonists chopped down the plentiful trees of America, cut them into lumber with hand tools, and exported to England whatever they did not use at home.

Left: The shells of old iron furnaces still stand in America.

Right: Once the sheep were washed and sheared, their wool had to be combed so the fibers could be spun into yarn. The process was called carding, after the wire brush called a "card."

Below: A reconstruction of a colonial furniture maker's workshop, and a selection of woodworking tools used during the 1700s.

state. The looming conflict accelerated the pace of American industrialization.

TO FIGHT A WAR

The American economy of 1775 relied on foreign trade. The war completely disrupted economic patterns. The Royal Navy blockaded the American coast to cut off imports and exports. Armies on campaign inflicted economic hardship by destroying buildings and bridges, seizing crops, cattle, and horses, and creating lawless regions overrun with deserters and bandits. When armies finished the campaign season and entered winter quarters, they acted like huge sponges soaking up local production and disrupting normal economic exchange.

Because of the British blockade, by necessity Americans turned to home manufacture to supply their domestic needs. In addition, military demands stimulated the weapons and munitions industries. Soldiers needed shelter and clothing, so manufacturers of tents, uniforms, and shoes expanded. Congress and several of the state governments provided special support for such manufacture. Supplies had to be transported

Below: British general Thomas Gage observed in 1768, "During my stay in Philadelphia, I could not help being surprised at the great increase of that city in buildings, mechanics, and manufacturers."

Opposite Bottom: Winters during the Revolutionary War were times of great hardship for American soldiers.

to the army, and that proved a boon for wagon makers, blacksmiths, and harness makers. Armies on both sides needed feeding, and that benefitted the agricultural industry. All of these manufacturing and transport activities required business skills. Many American merchants profited, and some failed disastrously.

When peace came, British goods again became available. They were better made and cheaper than the equivalent items made by domestic labor. Almost all of the home manufacture that had boomed during the war ended suddenly. American merchants found that others had replaced them in overseas markets. In addition, the new nation had accumulated a large war debt. Repaying the debt acted like a huge brake on the economy and caused political turmoil that persisted into the early 1790s.

Overall, from an economic standpoint the war years and the period of turmoil associated with the Confederation period were matched only by the Great Depression of 1929 to 1933. It is estimated that the American economy declined by nearly half between 1775 and 1790. In economic terms Americans paid a high price for their freedom.

Both armies used every available wagon to carry military supplies.

Insert below: In 1775 iron foundries in Massachusetts and Pennsylvania began casting artillery pieces and cannon balls for the rebel army.

AN INDEPENDENT NATION

During the time the American colonies fought for independence the Industrial Revolution in England rapidly accelerated. The most significant inventions for the English textile industry straddled the period of conflict: Richard Arkwright patented his water frame (see Volume 2) in 1769 and established a second patent for a series of machines that performed carding, **drawing**, and roving in 1775, the year when the American Minutemen started the war at Lexington and Concord; Samuel Crompton developed and perfected his mule (see Volume 2) between 1772 and 1777, the year the rebels won the decisive Battle of Saratoga. In 1776—the year the British Army hounded George Washington's men from New York City to the banks of the

One of the machines that changed the British textile industry—a carding engine—viewed from the side and the top. People once carded textile fibers by hand with a wire brush called a "card." The carding engine combed a higher volume of fiber in much less time.

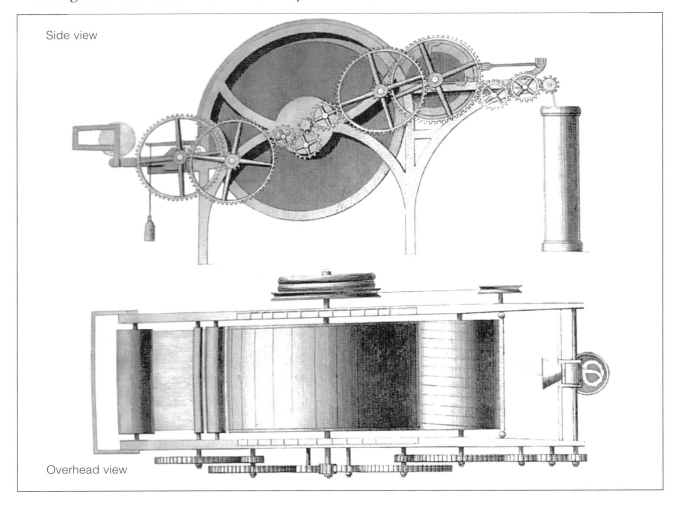

Side view

Overhead view

Delaware River—James Watt and his partners installed the first steam engine (see Volume 2) to provide the blast needed for a **coke**-fired blast furnace.

British industrialists and their political leaders were trying hard to maintain a monopoly over the inventions and innovations associated with the beginning of the Industrial Revolution. On the eve of and at the end of the war Parliament passed new laws to prevent the leakage of industrial secrets. An act of 1774 forbade the export of tools used to manufacture cotton and linen-cotton textiles. In 1781 Parliament tightened legislation to plug holes in the previous laws in an effort to prevent the escape of industrial drawings and models of machinery.

The United States emerged from the war farther behind than ever in the industrial race. Thomas Jefferson, who was much better informed about world events than most Americans, observed the situation first hand. He visited England after the war and reported with amazement that "Strange as it may appear," the English cotton manufacturers "card, spin, and even weave" by using water power. However, at least the infant nation did not confront the challenge of inventing the new machines. Rather, as Alexander Hamilton and others pointed out, the problem was to get hold of them.

A bold act of industrial espionage brought the revolution in textile manufacture to the United States. English-born Samuel Slater had begun working in childhood as an apprentice to the owner of a textile factory. A partner of the inventor Richard Arkwright, at one point took charge of young Slater's training. Slater himself showed great natural aptitude for mechanical invention.

Textile producers in the United States, forbidden access to machine drawings, began offering rewards to skilled textile workers who could help them reproduce British machinery.

Alexander Hamilton wanted to use the new power of America's central government to promote industry. In 1791 he issued his *Report on Manufactures*: "The Employment of Machinery forms an item of great importance in the general mass of national industry. It is an artificial force brought in aid of the natural force of man; and to all the purpose of labor, is an increase of hands, an accession of strength, unencumbered too by the expense of maintaining the laborer."

COKE: a form of coal that has been heated up to remove gases, so that it burns with great heat and little smoke

Left: Samuel Slater was so talented as an apprentice that he was placed in charge of mill machinery by the age of 17. When he left for America, he kept his destination secret. His farmer's disguise may have come naturally, as his father was a successful farmer.

THE MACHINES OF SLATER MILL

The machines of Slater Mill ran on water power. Water from the Blackstone River turned a huge waterwheel, and the rotation of the wheel turned gears. The gears then turned a drive shaft that ran down the center of the workshop. Drive belts connected each machine to the drive shaft. Mill buildings were long and narrow with windows along the sides, so that light from the windows reached the entire work area.

The first step was to feed the 500-pound bales of cotton into the bale-breaker. Cotton producers and sellers sometimes tried to cheat their customers by concealing rocks in the bales to make them weigh more, since customers paid by the pound. When the bale-breaker's heavy toothed drum spun around, the hidden rocks came flying out at any workers who had the misfortune to be nearby.

The next step was the carding engine, where another toothed drum, this time with much smaller teeth, combed and separated the cotton fibers. Note the leather drive belt.

The drawing frame drew the cotton fibers into a loose strand in preparation for spinning into thread.

Below: The thread was woven into cloth by home workers. A fly shuttle loom typical of those in use during the 1820s.

Above: The spinning frame spun multiple strands into cotton thread and wound it onto bobbins.

Twenty-one-year-old Samuel Slater seized the chance to come to the United States in 1789 and reap the financial rewards for his training and talent. He did not have to risk smuggling drawings into the country. He carried them in his head. He did, however, lie to British emigration authorities and claim he was a farmer to hide the fact that he was highly trained in all aspects of textile production. Slater was not the first skilled mechanic to defy the ban and come to America, but he was the first one capable of running a successful business.

Slater went to work for the Rhode Island company Almy and Brown. The company provided the money for him to build spinning and carding machines like the ones he carried in his memory. Slater hired skilled tradesmen, such as carpenters and millwrights, to build the machines he designed. The factory produced spun yarn that was "put out" to the local families who performed the weaving. After about ten years with Almy and Brown Slater began his own successful company and built

The original Slater Mill as it was built at Pawtucket, Rhode Island, in 1793 no longer exists, nor were any drawings made of it. This photograph was taken after the building had been enlarged and remodeled.

cotton mills in several New England locations. Meanwhile, the success of Slater's mill led to the construction of new mills throughout New England.

Initially most textile manufacture took place in small mills located in small New England villages that had reliable flowing water to power the machinery. The spinning mill was the economic center of such "mill villages." A mill employed no more than about 70 workers. Often entire family groups worked at the mill, or the adult men worked on farms owned by the mill owner.

Inside the mill adult men made up about one-third of the workers. They performed the skilled jobs, including hand loom weaving, machine maintenance, dyeing, and mule spinning. Operating a mule required considerable experience and so was more highly paid. A mule operator received a wage that sometimes exceeded the rate paid to overseers. Male workers also occupied all supervisory positions.

WATER FRAME: a water-powered frame for spinning cotton, one of the earliest machines invented for textile manufacture

Samuel Slater introduced the spinning mule to his mills around 1805. The mule, a British invention (see Volume 2), combined the advantages of two other inventions—the spinning jenny and the **water frame**—to produce a high-quality yarn. The child under the machine on the right has the job of piecing broken threads together.

Adult women made up about 40 percent of the work force. They operating the spinning machines and, after the introduction of power looms, ran those machines as well.

Children, usually the offspring of adults who worked at the mill, completed the work force. They performed a variety of unskilled tasks for which they received low wages. The yarn often broke during the spinning process. Children served as "piecers," splicing together broken strands of yarn as quickly as possible so the machine could resume its work. The mill owner "put out" the spun yarn to local households that, in turn, wove the yarn into cloth.

The small mill village was practically a self-contained world complete with other small industries like saw mills, tanneries, and blacksmith shops. But the mill itself, and its owner, dominated local economic life. He often built housing next to the mill and rented it out to families. The owner insisted that his workers attend church and even shop only in the village.

There were social advantages to a work environment where everyone knew one another, and entire families lived and worked together at the same place. The great potential disadvantage for the workers rested in the unchecked power of the mill owner. An unfair or corrupt owner could ruin a family's ability to support itself. He literally controlled their economic lifeblood. More often workers and owners in those small mill villages lived harmoniously, and the pattern of life that grew up around the mill became a familiar aspect of New England rural life.

Ahead lay a much different future when textile production moved inside large mills operating in urban landscapes.

Putting out system:
See also
Volume 1 pages 31, 51–52

Factory towns:
See also
Volume 10 page 39

The United States had more usable water-power sites than Great Britain. Typically, water was diverted from a stream and directed to fall onto a waterwheel (see water flowing from left). Water filled the spaces in the wheel, and the weight of the water turned the wheel. The turning wheel powered machinery in such places as New England textile factories, Maine sawmills, and Pennsylvania iron plantations.

THE DIFFUSION OF KNOWLEDGE

Samuel Slater was enormously successful, but many other English immigrants brought useful knowledge and skills. Customs data for the period 1773 to 1775 show that 500 men reported that they worked in the textile industry. A later sample taken between 1824 and 1831 lists 5,000 such British immigrants, including 153 textile machine workers. In the 1790s an American writer asserted that "a large proportion of the most successful manufacturers in the United States are persons, who were journeymen, and in a few instances were foremen in the work-shops and manufactories of Europe, who have been skillful, sober and frugal, and having thus saved a little money, have set up for themselves with great advantage in America."

One of Samuel Slater's early American spinning machines

THE PAPER INDUSTRY

Papermaking was a widespread American manufacturing activity, with about one-third of the total concentrated around Philadelphia. Colonial paper was made from linen rags soaked in water and beaten by a water-powered trip-hammer until reduced to pulp. Workers spread the pulp into thin layers on rectangular frames until it partially dried. Then they placed the sheets between layers of felt and pressed them to squeeze out all of the water.

Around 1780 the industry began to modernize and within eight years had made impressive progress. A Frenchman who visited the American paper mills in 1788 commented, "Their process in making paper is much simpler than ours." He added that American quality seemed to match French quality. By 1797 no fewer than 60 paper mills operated along the banks of Brandywine Creek east of Philadelphia. Papermaking remained a handicraft industry until the 1840s, when it became mechanized in factories.

During colonial times the typical print shop was owned and operated by craftsmen called "master printers." They used large, heavy wooden presses imported from England and hand-set small metal pieces with raised lettering to create words and sentences. It was tedious work, and the physical effort to manipulate the lever that lowered and raised the press required considerable strength. Colonial printers were

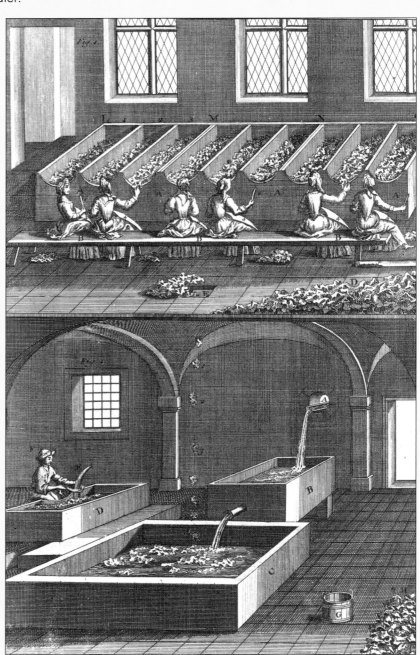

The first step in the papermaking process: workers sorted linen rags and put them to soak and ferment in large tanks of water.

noted for their unique gait caused by muscular overdevelopment on their right sides since the right arm operated the lever. Two competent pressmen could print 240 sheets of paper per hour.

All the equipment and supplies required by a printer—presses, tables, frames, ink, paper—made the printing business capital-intensive. To consider being a printer, a man needed a fair sum to invest. Consequently, colonial printers—like other urban craft masters such as silversmiths and carpet weavers—stood solidly in the economic middle class. One could not be poor and expect to set up a print shop. Because of the high costs associated with the business, particularly metal type and paper, printers seldom grew wealthy.

During the early 1800s Philadelphia became the center of the American printing industry. In 1800 a Philadelphia printer introduced iron presses manufactured in America. That breakthrough ended dependence on imported printing presses. As time passed, the combination of cheaper paper and improved printing techniques allowed the growth of low-priced daily newspapers for the local market and weeklies for the national market. In turn, such publications helped spread technical knowledge and thus did their part in spreading the Industrial Revolution in America.

On the right a worker is spreading the linen pulp on a frame, the next step on the path from linen rags to a sheet of paper. By 1787 more than 60 paper mills were operating in the United States. Steam power was first used in paper manufacture in 1816.

In spite of British efforts to retain the early secrets of the Industrial Revolution, the United States, like nations in western Europe, managed to acquire technical information. Quite simply there was too much money to be made by discovering technical secrets, and consequently men found a way to do so. Among many the British consul for the middle American states worked hard to block technology transfer. He discovered two Englishmen who smuggled one carding and three spinning machines from Liverpool to Philadelphia "packed in Queen's ware [dinner service dishes] crates and casks, to elude discovery." A combination of immigrant mechanics, American visits to England to tour factories, drawings and descriptions obtained legally or by smuggling, the import of entire machines, and last but not least, the native ingenuity of American mechanics delivered to the United States the necessary information to industrialize.

The European wars fought between 1792 and 1815 interrupted trade. The conflict even drew in America, which

Around 1790 Jacob Perkins of Massachusetts invented a nail-making machine that cut out the nails and formed their heads in one operation. Mass-produced nails were both cheaper to make and easier for a carpenter to drive with his hammer.

During the War of 1812 the British and U.S. navies battled for control of the sea and of oceangoing trade.

fought the War of 1812 against Great Britain. As had occurred in the Revolutionary War, the British navy blockaded the American coast. During the war period industry in the United States mostly had to rely on its own resources. This isolation provided one advantage: It created a protected market for American manufacture.

During the Industrial Revolution new industries had trouble competing with established industries. For example, the well-established British textile industry could usually outcompete a newly established textile industry somewhere else. Countries typically passed legislation, such as high tariffs (taxes) on imports, to protect an infant industry against British competition. The 1808 decision by President Thomas Jefferson to **embargo** English goods, followed by the British blockade during the War of 1812, served the same purpose.

EMBARGO: a wartime measure to restrict trade in certain goods or prohibit all movement by trading ships

The cotton mills of Pawtucket, Rhode Island, stood at the falls of the Blackstone River about five miles from Providence. The workers of this small community were the first to run the new cotton-spinning machinery in the United States.

OLIVER EVANS: AN AMERICAN INVENTOR

Oliver Evans was born in 1755. When he was a young teenager, his father apprenticed him to a wheelwright. The boy learned how to build devices using both wood and metal. During his early twenties he carefully watched how local gristmills operated and conceived of several ways to make them more efficient. He resolved to implement them at a Delaware mill he owned.

He devised a water-powered "grain elevator," a long, continuous leather belt holding a series of small buckets, to haul the grain to the mill. This machine did the work normally performed by two strong men. Overlooked at the time was the use of a leather belt rather than gears to transmit power. Later, leather belting used in that way became widespread in American factories.

Evans also invented what he called a "hopper boy" (since the machine did the work normally done by a boy), which was a 12-foot-long, water-powered, revolving rake that spread the ground meal evenly so that it could dry and then raked the meal into a hopper from where it could be sifted.

The two devices reduced the labor needed to operate a gristmill from four men and a boy to two men. At first American mills were slow to adopt his inventions. However, between 1800 and 1840 almost all new mills and many older ones employed grain elevators and hopper boys. Because American patent law at that time offered weak protection for inventors, Evans did not personally profit very much.

Continued on page 38

Top: Oliver Evans investigated new solutions to old problems from the time he was a teenage apprentice until shortly before his death in 1819.

Left: Among Oliver Evans's many inventions were two machines to mechanize one of the nation's most important industries, flour milling. One was the "hopper boy." The other, shown here, was the automated grain elevator.

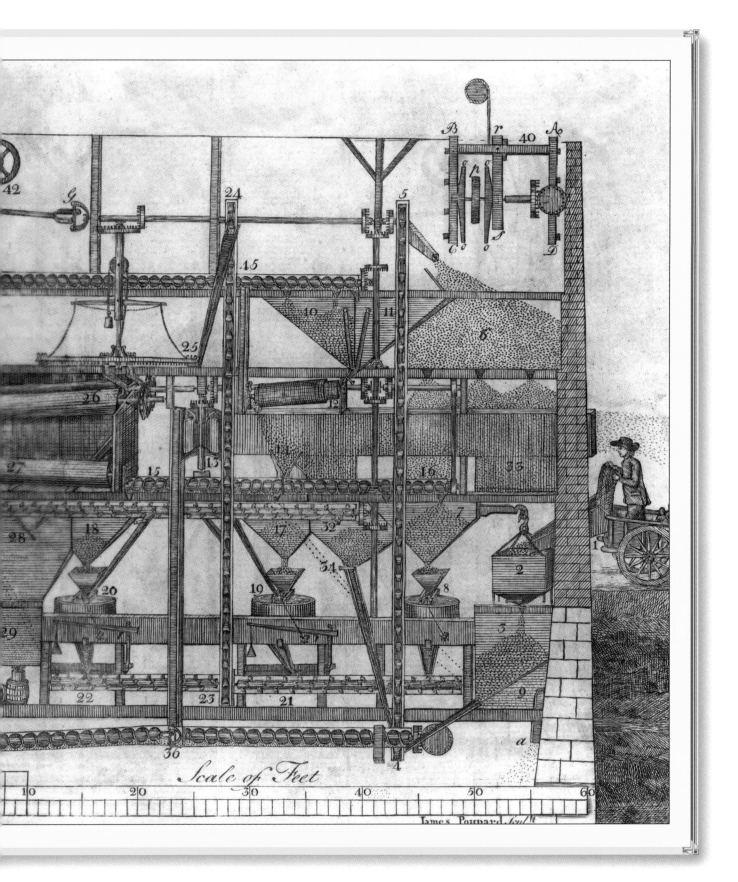

Scale of Feet

James Poupard. Sculp.

Meanwhile, during the 1780s Evans began experimenting with high-pressure steam engines. By 1801 he had built such an engine to power a grinding mill designed to pulverize plaster of Paris. Five years later an Evans engine, which the inventor accurately described as simple, cheap, and durable, was installed in a Kentucky gristmill. That success led to the construction of a steam flour mill in Pittsburgh. The two facilities were among the first in the United States to use steam for manufacturing.

Evans also made an enduring contribution to the American Industrial Revolution by developing a machine shop in Philadelphia to manufacture his engines and another in Pittsburgh to build steamboats. The Philadelphia site employed 35 workers and included an iron foundry with two furnaces, a blacksmith shop, a millstone manufacturing plant, and a steam engine workshop.

When early American inventors such as Robert Fulton needed engines, they purchased them from England. Evans's machine shops, and those operated by a handful of likeminded men, served to train a generation of American-born machine builders and draftsmen. Consequently, by 1820 the need to look to England for machines and mechanics was on the decline and by 1840 had ended.

America's Industrial Revolution expanded very quickly in large part because of its skilled, innovative machine tool industry, one that Evans was instrumental in founding.

Below: Oliver Evans's high-pressure steam engine was smaller and lighter than the one developed in Great Britain by James Watt. This was just what he intended, because he was particularly interested in building what he called "steam carriages" to carry freight.

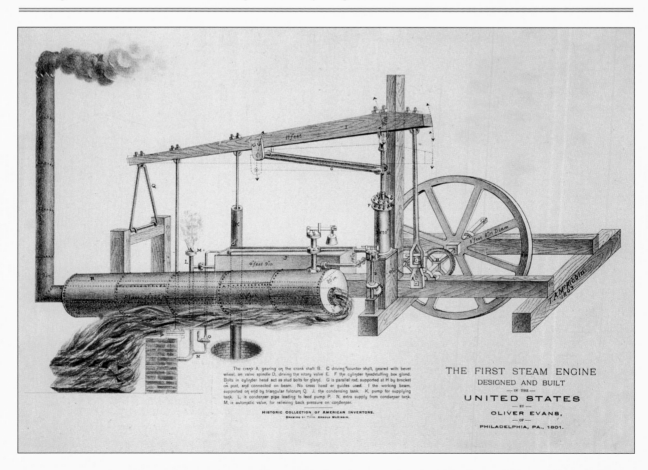

THE FIRST STEAM ENGINE
DESIGNED AND BUILT
— IN THE —
UNITED STATES
— BY —
OLIVER EVANS,
— OF —
PHILADELPHIA, PA., 1801.

Right: Although Evans's idea for a steam carriage did not bear fruit, in 1805 he did build the *Oruktor Amphibolos*, a huge, lumbering steam-propelled dredge that moved on both land and water.

Below: A reconstruction of a 19th-century American machine shop

Between 1808 and 1812 some 36 cotton mills and 41 woolen mills began operation. A New England merchant wrote in 1810, "Our people have 'cotton mill fever' as it is called. Every place almost occupied with cotton mills...spinning yarn and making cloth is become our greatest business." Once the war began, the trend accelerated. By 1813, 76 cotton mills were operating within a 30-mile radius of Providence, Rhode Island, alone.

When the war ended in 1815, American manufacturers lost their artificial protection from British competition. Because they are light in weight, textiles can be shipped long distances without incurring high freight costs. British manufacturers took advantage; and just as had occurred after the Revolutionary War, merchant ships sailed from Great Britain laden with cheap textiles to dump on the American market. Many American mills went bankrupt.

American manufacturers sought one key to survival against British competition—the acquisition of the latest industrial technology. A manufacturer named E.I. Du Pont established a woolen mill in Delaware in 1816. Du Pont advertised in Philadelphia newspapers for "any person lately arrived from Europe, and well acquainted with some branch in the finishing department of a CLOTH FACTORY." Du Pont hoped that a recent ("lately arrived") immigrant would possess state-of-the-art knowledge.

British efforts to retain industrial secrets, Jefferson's 1808 embargo, and the subsequent War of 1812 all worked to slow the arrival of the latest British textile inventions. But inevitably they came to America; and (as is described in Volume 5) when combined with the

A dress made in the United States during the early 1800s out of cotton imported from Great Britain.

energy and vision provided by Francis Cabot Lowell, new mills on a scale never before seen in America launched a new era in the American Industrial Revolution.

ELI WHITNEY AND THE AMERICAN SYSTEM

When the Massachusetts inventor Eli Whitney undertook a contract to supply the U.S. government with 10,000 muskets, he faced a formidable challenge. Musket manufacture involved an enormous amount of hand labor, with each component requiring hand tooling and hand assembly. Whitney conceived of a way to accelerate the production process by using power-driven machines to mass produce each component using narrow **tolerances** that would allow components to be interchangeable. In other words, the trigger on one musket could equally well fire another musket.

Whitney described his goal in a letter: "...to form the tools so the tools themselves shall fashion the work and give to every part its just proportion—which when once accomplished, will give expedition [increased efficiency], uniformity, and exactness to the whole." Whitney's insight gave rise to the "American system," which took a complex manufacturing process and broke it into a series of small, easily repeated elements. The key to this approach was the construction of precise machine tools that could produce interchangeable parts. Interchangeable parts simplified the process of assembly and repair since assemblers did not have to match parts that could only fit one unique partner, and repairers did not have to grind and file replacements in order to make repairs.

Machine tools:
See also
Volume 3 pages 4–9

TOLERANCE: the amount by which an object can deviate from a standard size or shape

Handmade rifle (top) and musket, both used during the Revolutionary War.

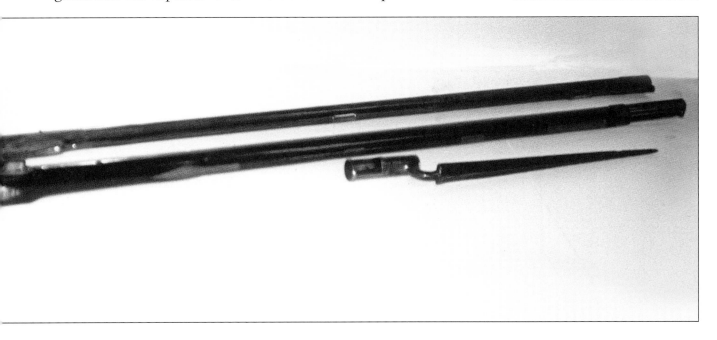

Guns made with interchangeable parts were more expensive than those made without such parts. However, cost was not the major concern for the military since its goal was the ability to repair weapons in the field. Consequently, other inventors took Whitney's ideas and established their own gun factories. By 1817 James Hall was successfully machine manufacturing guns at the federal arsenal at Harpers Ferry, Virginia, where he installed an improved milling machine that cut metal with unprecedented accuracy. Five years later Hall reported, "I have succeeded in establishing methods for fabricating arms exactly alike, & with perfect economy, by the hands of common workmen."

Harpers Ferry Armory: Gun manufacture reached the heights of technical excellence at the Springfield and Harpers Ferry armories, where muskets were assembled from precisely machined, interchangeable parts.

REGULATING THE WORK

In order to ensure that each component was made the same, workers built a so-called pattern piece, a model weapon constructed to great accuracy and precision. The model provided the pattern for mass production. Skilled craftsmen took the patterns of individual components and made a complex system of **jigs** and similar devices that held the work in place so holes could be drilled and edges cut in exactly the same place time after time.

An inspector used measures called "go or no go" gauges to assess quickly if the component had been properly made. Either it fit correctly in the gauge ("go"), or it did not ("no

JIG: a pattern piece, usually of metal, used as a guide for shaping and duplicating an object with a power tool

ELI WHITNEY

Eli Whitney is most remembered for inventing a cotton gin, but his contribution to mass production had an equally important influence on American economic life.

Eli Whitney was born in Massachusetts in 1765. From an early age he showed a curiosity about machines. While in his early teens, he built a workshop on his family's farm. There he began a small manufacturing business making nails, hinges, and other metal objects that were in short supply during the Revolutionary War. After the war he resumed his education and graduated from Yale in 1792.

He went to work as a tutor in Savannah, Georgia, and became interested in the local cotton economy. Planters produced a cotton loaded with seeds tightly embedded in the fiber balls. Removing the seeds was a labor-intensive, and therefore expensive, process. In 1793 Whitney invented a device, called a "cotton gin," that used a rotating toothed metal cylinder operated by a crank to remove the seeds. He called it a "cotton gin." His cotton gin allowed planters to reassign slaves from cleaning cotton to planting and harvesting. As a result, cotton production in the United States expanded tremendously and helped supply a growing American cotton textile industry.

American patent law was not yet enforceable, so Whitney had to watch as others copied his invention and manufactured it themselves.

In 1798 he obtained a federal contract to deliver 10,000 muskets. At that time each musket was a handmade specialty item. Whitney devised a method of mass production that later became known as "the American system." (See pages 41-52.) Whitney's concept had profound implications for manufacturing and became the model for industrial production in the United States, but it did little to help him fulfill his contract. He delivered the muskets nine years later than his contract called for, and they were manufactured without interchangeable parts!

Whitney's cotton gin was operated with a hand crank that turned a toothed drum. The teeth gripped the cotton fibers and fed them through an opening too small to let in the seeds. One slave turning the crank did the work once done by many slaves picking the seed out by hand. Cotton was first planted in America in 1621 but did not become a major crop until after the Revolutionary War. It can be argued that the cotton gin influenced the course of American history by making the slave-holding plantations of the South more profitable.

go"). Either the holes lined up, or they did not. Using such gauges, an inspector maintained a high level of quality control.

Years after Eli Whitney's death his concept for a new method of production was triumphantly demonstrated when a British delegation visited the Springfield Armory. Workers tore apart 10 muskets manufactured between 1844 and 1853 and thoroughly mixed their parts. They then fitted them back together, and all 10 worked perfectly.

After the two U.S. armories had perfected their manufacturing processes, Americans called the use of special-purpose machines operated by unskilled workers and the division of labor "armory

An arms inspector used these gauges to evaluate the quality of model 1841 rifles.

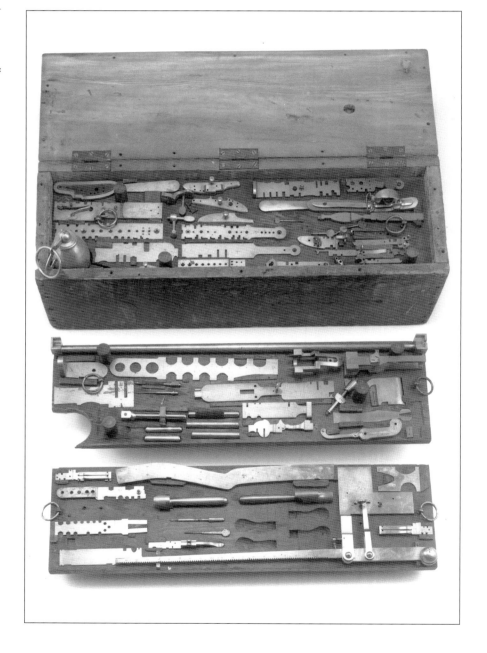

practice." The British inspectors who visited the Springfield Armory called it "the American system of manufacture," and the label stuck. The "American system" became the foundation for mass production for the mass market.

CLOCK MAKING

Armory practice spread to other industries such as clock making. Traditional clock makers could make four or five clocks a year. Consequently, clocks were expensive, costing $50 if made with brass wheels and gears and $25 if fabricated with wood.

In 1802 a master clock maker named Eli Terry built a factory in Connecticut that used a waterwheel to power some of the manufacturing processes. Output climbed to 200 clocks a year. A few years later Terry simplified the entire manufacturing process so that special machine tools made some of the parts. Production rates increased tenfold.

By 1830 numerous factories in Connecticut and neighboring Massachusetts used machine power to produce wooden clocks. Some manufacturers even used interchangeable parts. After 1837 locally manufactured, high-quality sheet brass became available, so some of the manufacturers switched to brass wheels for their wooden clocks. That switch, in turn, led to the development of more sophisticated die-stamping machinery.

A clock with wooden works manufactured by Eli Terry around 1815

AMERICA'S INDUSTRIAL PIONEERS

THOMAS BLANCHARD: 1788–1864

Born in Massachusetts. Blanchard began inventing things as a boy, including an apple peeler that could have been a forerunner to his famous lathe. He invented the gunstock-turning lathe in 1819 while working for Springfield Arsenal. His design was widely pirated despite the fact that he had a patent.

A screw lathe in a reconstructed 1870s machine shop. A lathe shaped standardized objects by using a pattern to turn each object against a fixed cutting tool. The principle behind the lathe was applied to other objects besides gunstocks.

ELEUTHERE IRENEE DUPONT: 1771–1834

Dupont emigrated from France to New York City in 1800. Having worked at a gunpowder factory in France, he established a gunpowder mill in Delaware in 1802 and later a woolen mill. His gunpowder mill proved very profitable during the War of 1812. His business became the famous E.I. DuPont de Nemours and Company.

OLIVER EVANS: 1755–1819

Born in Delaware, Evans began his apprenticeship to a wheelwright at the age of 16 and started his long career as an inventor. His creations include a machine for making textile-carding devices, an automated grist mill, and the high-pressure steam engine, which—beginning in 1801—he applied to many uses.

JACOB PERKINS: 1766–1849

Perkins was born in Massachusetts. Like many other inventors, Perkins failed to profit from his 1790 nail machine because of patent disputes. He later developed a means of engraving currency that made it harder to counterfeit; but failing to interest Americans in the process, he moved to England and ran a successful business engraving banknotes and postage stamps. Perkins also developed improvements to high-pressure steam boilers and other aspects of steamboat design.

Belmont Nail Works, Wheeling, West Virginia. Nails were once cut by hand, one at a time, from iron rods. Jacob Perkins's nail machine changed production from a cottage industry to mass-produced factory work.

SAMUEL SLATER: 1768–1835

Born in England, Slater was apprenticed to a textile factory where he showed great aptitude for improving the machinery. He came to Boston in 1789 and used his special knowledge of textile machinery to work in Rhode Island for Almy and Brown. In 1798 he went out on his own and built textile mills throughout New England.

ELI TERRY: 1772–1852

Born in Connecticut, Terry was apprenticed to clockmaker at age of 14 and eventually opened his own clock factory. His factory used water-powered machines to mass-produce clocks with interchangeable wooden parts. His clock design of 1814 was the basis for the production of more than 10,000 clocks a year.

ELI WHITNEY: 1765–1825

While still a teenager Whitney set up a business on his family's Massachusetts farm and made nails and metal tools, which were in great demand during the Revolutionary War. He graduated from Yale in 1792 and went to work as a tutor in Georgia. There he invented the cotton gin, but despite having a patent, he failed to profit from his invention because imitators competed with him. Whitney then went into gun manufacturing in New England and pioneered techniques of mass production.

By the mid-1800s wooden clock mechanisms had been replaced by brass.

The adoption of armory practice was so successful that by 1850 an average clock-making factory produced between 130,000 and 150,000 clocks per year, and the price had fallen to $1.50.

REGULATING THE WORKER

The federal armories led the way in the manufacture and use of interchangeable parts, and later Samuel Colt took the same approach to make his famous Colt revolvers. Over time the idea of uniform manufacture of interchangeable parts spread to other industries.

Mass production changed worker's lives. For example, prior to the introduction of the American system of manufacture skilled craftsmen made each component for each gun. Not only did the American system lead to greater division of labor, it also brought the invention of special-purpose machines to make accurate, interchangeable parts. In 1819 a mechanic named Thomas Blanchard invented a gunstock-turning **lathe**. His device copied a pattern piece and was able to rapidly produce irregular wooden objects like gunstocks. Within six years Blanchard invented 14 machines that largely mechanized gunstock manufacture.

Not only could a gunstock be turned out in only 22 minutes (after which time a small amount of hand labor completed the assembly), but Blanchard's machines did not require highly skilled operators. Blanchard hired "men and boys at very low wages, that know little or nothing of the business" and set them to work at his machines. Skilled workers complained, of course, since they worried about declining wages or even

Opposite: Thomas Blanchard's gunstock-turning lathe and a milling machine that cut precisely measured metal parts for guns.

Lathes:
See also
Volume 1 page 12
Volume 4 pages 50–51

LATHE: a machine for shaping pieces of wood or metal, which works by rapidly turning the material against a stationary cutting edge

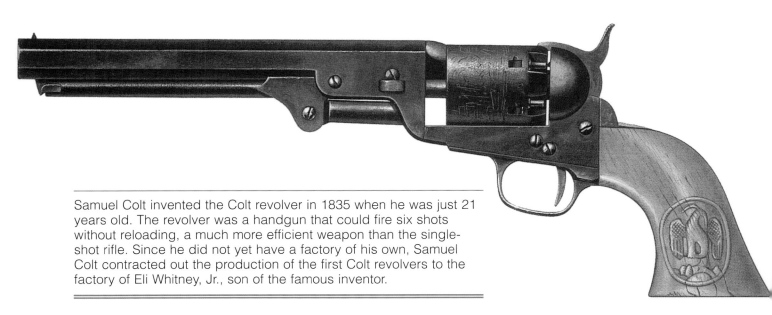

Samuel Colt invented the Colt revolver in 1835 when he was just 21 years old. The revolver was a handgun that could fire six shots without reloading, a much more efficient weapon than the single-shot rifle. Since he did not yet have a factory of his own, Samuel Colt contracted out the production of the first Colt revolvers to the factory of Eli Whitney, Jr., son of the famous inventor.

losing their jobs entirely; but the economic advantages of the American system trumped their protests. The Springfield Armory in Massachusetts changed from a large craft shop that had little division of labor in 1800 into a mass production factory with 36 different operational specialities in 1815, 100 in 1825, and 400 by 1855, with each one paying its own wage.

THE IRON INDUSTRY

The United States was slow to adopt the great improvements that had taken place in the British iron industry between 1750 and 1800. While coke-fired blast furnaces dominated British production by the turn of the century, the first successful coke furnace did not open in the United States until 1837. In part, American ironmasters did not use coke because the available eastern coal was unsuited to making it. Furthermore, because of the presence of cheap, abundant timber charcoal remained the preferred fuel until about 1850. Only the gradual depletion of forests in the eastern United States and an increased demand for iron products caused the switch to coal. Likewise, American ironmasters were slow to replace forge hammers with more modern rolling mills. In large part, ironmasters based their decision on the fact that abundant waterpower allowed them to purify pig iron by using forge hammers. As late as 1817, 34 years after the rolling mill had been patented in England, and at a time when British producers had clearly demonstrated its superior power and efficiency, a traveler in the United States observed, "...nowhere that I know among our iron works, have iron cylinder rollers been substituted for the tilt hammer."

Finally, a 20-year period between about 1820 and 1840 witnessed American manufacturers adopting the full range of British innovations. For example, in 1828 a rolling and nail mill on the Schuylkill River in Pennsylvania employed over 600 workers.

American consumers wanted iron for stoves and for farm and household implements. Local furnaces fulfilled much of this demand.

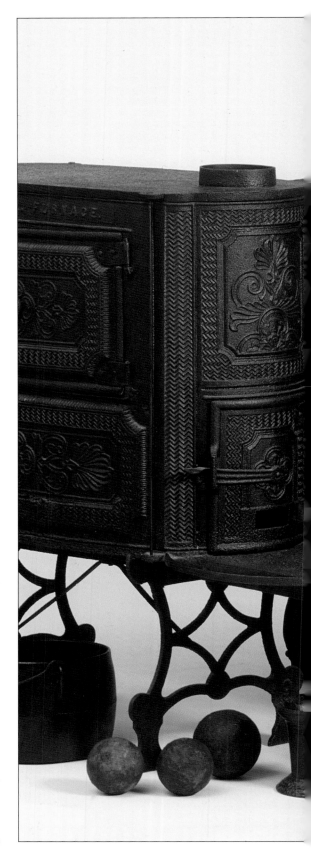

EARLY SOCIAL PERSPECTIVE

American propaganda before and during the war had presented a picture of the evil British wallowing in vice. In opposition stood American virtue. As Americans pondered the consequences of industrialization, many worried that it would bring British vices like the poor working and living conditions seen in Manchester and would reduce the free American worker to a mere cog in the industrial machine. Political leaders who agreed with Thomas Jefferson's view of the American future, namely, a rural, agricultural nation filled

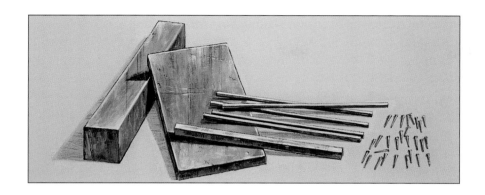

Rolling mills used heavy rollers to convert heated iron bars into sheets. At slitting mills the sheets were reheated and cut into thin strips, which in turn were cut into nails.

Thomas Jefferson fervently believed that a virtuous, representative government had to be based on free, independent farmers. He argued that Europe could and should fulfill America's need for manufactured goods.

with virtuous farmers, opposed policies to encourage industry. Jefferson himself wrote, "Let us never wish to see our citizens occupied at a work-bench."

Many people thought that industrialization, particularly the factory system, would make workers lose interest in their jobs. What was worse, they feared, would be a loss of national virtues like frugality, simplicity, and independence. Whether Americans had ever possessed such virtues in unusual numbers was debatable, but what was certain was that the British landscape and its people had changed because of the Industrial Revolution. Some prominent American thinkers did not want to see such change come to their country.

The newly independent United States had to adjust to a new economic reality. Despite all the complaints about the mother country, England had provided some significant economic advantages. As long as it remained a colony, America had enjoyed lower import and export duties (taxes). England had also served as a source of investment and credit. The Royal Navy had protected American merchant ships against all enemies. After 1781 those advantages were gone.

Below: An American boiler factory in Charlestown, MA. in the early 1800s.

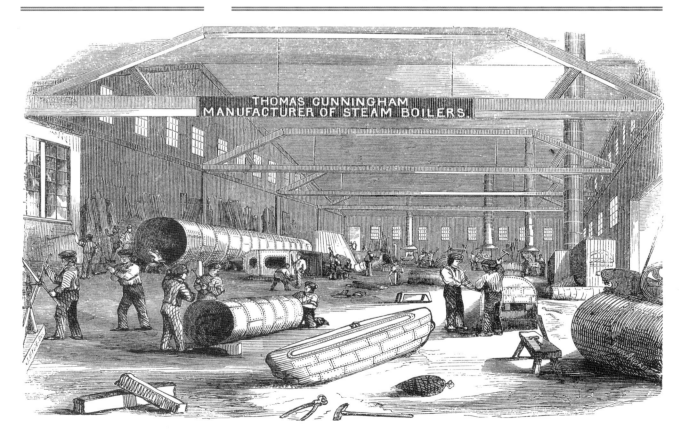

THOMAS CUNNINGHAM
MANUFACTURER OF STEAM BOILERS.

1810: AN INDUSTRIAL SNAPSHOT

In 1810 a gifted civil servant and merchant banker named Tench Coxe took government census figures on national manufacturing and provided some statistical analysis. In spite of gaps and omissions, that data provides the best available view of American industry at the time.

Among goods manufactured outside of the home, flour milling led the way. The production of leather goods such as harnesses, saddles, boots, and shoes was second and exceeded iron and steel production by more than 30 percent. Third in rank order was the manufacture of food products, including liquors, while iron and steel were fourth.

A wide gap existed between those top four ranking activities and the next leading sector, the manufacture of all types of machinery. Wood products followed machinery, with the manufacture of hats and chemicals providing the only other major categories of industrial manufacture. Because most textiles were made at home, they were not included on the list.

In rank order the state with the most manufacturing activity was Pennsylvania, followed by New York, Massachusetts, and Virginia, with Maryland and Connecticut vying for the fifth position.

Cotton factories in Lancashire, northwest England

ONE NATION, TWO ECONOMIES

The economies of the North and South began developing in different directions long before the Revolutionary War led to the creation of the United States. The southern colonies—Virginia, North Carolina, South Carolina, and Georgia—had the warmest climate and the richest soil. Wealthy colonists amassed huge plantations, some with thousands of acres. They also acquired plantations in the southern and coastal regions of Maryland and Delaware. The wealthiest planters owned dozens, even hundreds, of slaves to plant, cultivate, and harvest labor-intensive cash crops such as tobacco, rice, indigo, and—later—cotton. The economy of the southern colonies relied on the sale of these few commodities. The proceeds from these sales in turn purchased many of the necessities and luxuries of life. An early northern governor noted that plantation owners were so dedicated to planting cash crops "that they had rather buy food at very dear rates than produce it" themselves.

The southern population was thinly scattered across the land, so the South lacked the concentration of workers or customers necessary for industrial development. Unlike the colonies to the north, the southern colonies had only one major city, the port of Charles Town, South Carolina. With most capital invested in land and slaves, southerners had little to invest in industry. Consequently, the south lagged far behind the north in industrial development. Most industrial production was limited to plantation forges and workshops where slaves made such objects as tools, horseshoes, bricks, and lumber.

Two American rivers put to different uses: A southern cotton plantation (above) on the Mississippi River had ready access to steamboats for shipping the crop to market. The power of falling water attracted northern factory builders to the riverbanks of New England (below).

The northern colonies—Pennsylvania, New Jersey, New York, Connecticut, Rhode Island, Massachusetts, and New Hampshire—had a colder climate and shorter growing season. They became home to family farms worked by the owners, their families, and indentured servants or paid laborers. Successful northern farmers grew enough food for their own households and surplus food, grain, and livestock for sale. They could make enough money to live comfortably, but few could become rich.

The New England colonies had a large population and a small land area compared to the other colonies. With little land to pass on to their children, farmers apprenticed their sons to tradesmen in towns to learn skilled trades. So began the shift from farming to other occupations and the movement of the northern population from farms to towns. Such businesses as iron forges, tinsmiths, clock makers, and gunsmiths became commonplace in northern towns.

Ports, market towns, and seats of government grew into cities. The cities attracted both businesses and workers. Workers came both from nearby farms and from overseas. As the colonies became states and then formed a nation, immigrants came to work in the factories of northern cities, hoping to earn enough money to buy their own homes and farms. Meanwhile, southern plantations turned to growing cotton and sold much of it to textile mills in the North. Despite such economic interdependence, the two regions' divergent ways of life—and ultimately the South's reliance on slavery—led to political disagreement and civil war.

Much of industry increased its output dramatically to support the army during the Civil War. A New York foundry making Union cannons.

The southern states relied heavily on slave labor, particularly in cotton farming. By 1860 the population of the United States included 4 million slaves. A family of slaves in front of their cabin.

CONCLUSION

Beginning in colonial times, American industrialists adapted manufacturing practices to local conditions and to take advantage of local resources. Clock-makers built moving parts out of wood instead of metal because wood was widely available and cheap. Iron masters used charcoal instead of coke for the same reason. Metal workers used trip-hammers instead of rolling mills because water power was so abundant.

Often such practices persisted long after technical advances elsewhere, particularly in England, had changed and modernized European practices. Visitors who compared England and America often thought that American practices were old-fashioned or even obsolete. What they, and many subsequent historians, failed to realize was that American technicians often had chosen techniques and tools to make the best use of local resources.

For the same reason some technical advances that originated in the United States were slow to catch on elsewhere. Oliver Evans's machinery for gristmills and Jacob Perkins's nail machine are two examples of state-of-the-art designs that made little initial impact in England and thereafter were only slowly adopted. Likewise, a brass and iron tempering method developed by Nathan Sellers of Philadelphia in the 1780s took more than 10 years to spread to England. When his grandson visited British industrial sites in 1832, he commented that British ironworking facilities had old-fashioned machinery for large-scale operation compared to American facilities!

By 1825 the first phase of the American Industrial Revolution had ended. In that year Thomas Jefferson observed,

Grist mills, at which grain was ground into flour by water-powered millstones, dotted the American countryside.

"Our manufactures are now very nearly on a footing with those of England. She has not a single improvement which we do not possess, and many of them better adapted by ourselves to our ordinary use."

In the large northeastern cities a number of industries had blossomed, most notably iron and machine tool production around Philadelphia and textiles around Providence and Boston.

CHARCOAL-MAKING IN EARLY AMERICA

Charcoal is the word used to describe chunks of black carbon made by partially burning wood. It is used to build extra hot fires. The first step in making charcoal is to stack the wood.

Industry had reached a sufficient density so that entrepreneurs, inventors, technicians, and workers could meet and exchange ideas. The continuous transfer of information led both to the rapid spread of new machinery, tools, and ideas, and to the development of entirely new ways of doing things.

The American Industrial Revolution had reached a point where it was self-sustaining and ready for even more rapid expansion.

As the wood burns, dirt is piled over it to prevent air from getting to the fire. This makes the wood burn more slowly, so it just chars and does not get totally consumed by the fire.

The charcoal is removed from beneath the dirt pile.

A DATELINE OF MAJOR EVENTS DURING THE INDUSTRIAL REVOLUTION

BEFORE 1750	1760	1770	1780

REVOLUTIONS IN INDUSTRY AND TECHNOLOGY

1619: English settlers establish the first iron works in colonial America, near Jamestown, Virginia.

1689: Thomas Savery (England) patents the first design for a steam engine.

1709: Englishman Abraham Darby uses coke instead of coal to fuel his blast furnace.

1712: Englishman Thomas Newcomen builds the first working steam engine.

1717: Thomas Lombe establishes a silk-throwing factory in England.

1720: The first Newcomen steam engine on the Continent is installed at a Belgian coal mine.

1733: James Kay (England) invents the flying shuttle.

1742: Benjamin Huntsman begins making crucible steel in England.

1756: The first American coal mine opens.

1764: In England James Hargreaves invents the spinning jenny.

1769: Englishman Richard Arkwright patents his spinning machine, called a water frame.

James Watt of Scotland patents an improved steam engine design.

Josiah Wedgwood (England) opens his Etruria pottery works.

1771: An industrial spy smuggles drawings of the spinning jenny from England to France.

1774: John Wilkinson (England) builds machines for boring cannon cylinders.

1775: Arkwright patents carding, drawing, and roving machines.

In an attempt to end dependence on British textiles American revolutionaries open a spinning mill in Philadelphia using a smuggled spinning-jenny design.

1777: Oliver Evans (U.S.) invents a card-making machine.

1778: John Smeaton (England) introduces cast iron gearing to transfer power from waterwheels to machinery.

The water closet (indoor toilet) is invented in England.

1779: Englishman Samuel Crompton develops the spinning mule.

1783: Englishman Thomas Bell invents a copper cylinder to print patterns on fabrics.

1784: Englishman Henry Cort invents improved rollers for rolling mills and the puddling process for refining pig iron.

Frenchman Claude Berthollet discovers that chlorine can be used as a bleach.

The ironworks at Le Creusot use France's first rotary steam engine to power its hammers, as well as using the Continent's first coke-fired blast furnace.

1785: Englishman Edmund Cartwright invents the power loom.

1788: The first steam engine is imported into Germany.

REVOLUTIONS IN TRANSPORTATION AND COMMUNICATION

1757: The first canal is built in England.

Locks on an English canal

1785: The first canal is built in the United States, at Richmond, Virginia.

1787: John Fitch and James Rumsey (U.S.) each succeed in launching a working steamboat.

SOCIAL REVOLUTIONS

1723: Britain passes an act to allow the establishment of workhouses for the poor.

1750: The enclosure of common land gains momentum in Britain.

1776: Scottish professor Adam Smith publishes *The Wealth of Nations*, which promotes laissez-faire capitalism.

The workhouse

INTERNATIONAL RELATIONS

Continental Army in winter quarters at Valley Forge

1775–1783: The American Revolution. Thirteen colonies win their independence from Great Britain and form a new nation, the United States of America.

1789–1793: The French Revolution leads to abolition of the monarchy and execution of the king and queen. Mass executions follow during the Reign of Terror, 1793–1794.

1790	**1800**	**1810**	**1820**

1790: English textile producer Samuel Slater begins setting up America's first successful textile factory in Pawtucket, Rhode Island.

Jacob Perkins (U.S.) invents a machine capable of mass-producing nails.

1791: French chemist Nicholas Leblanc invents a soda-making process.

1793: Eli Whitney (U.S.) invents a cotton gin.

1794: Germany's first coke-fired blast furnace is built.

The first German cotton spinning mill installs Arkwright's water frame.

1798: Eli Whitney devises a system for using power-driven machinery to produce interchangeable parts, the model for the "American System" of manufacture.

Wool-spinning mills are built in Belgium using machinery smuggled out of England.

A cylindrical papermaking machine is invented in England.

1801: American inventor Oliver Evans builds the first working high-pressure steam engine and uses it to power a mill.

Joseph-Marie Jacquard (France) invents a loom that uses punch cards to produce patterned fabrics.

A cotton-spinning factory based on British machinery opens in Belgium.

The first cotton-spinning mill in Switzerland begins operation.

Austria establishes the Continent's largest cotton-spinning mill.

1802: In England William Murdock uses coal gas to light an entire factory.

Richard Trevithick builds a high-pressure steam engine in England.

1807: British businessmen open an industrial complex in Belgium that includes machine manufacture, coal mining, and iron production.

1808: Russia's first spinning mill begins production in Moscow.

1810: Henry Maudslay (England) invents the precision lathe.

1816: Steam power is used for the first time in an American paper mill.

English scientist Humphry Davy invents a safety lamp for coal miners in England.

1817: The French iron industry's first puddling works and rolling mills are established.

1819: Thomas Blanchard (U.S.) invents a gunstock-turning lathe, which permits production of standardized parts.

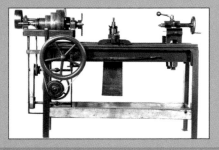

A turning lathe

1821: Massachusetts businessmen begin developing Lowell as a site for textile mills.

1822: Power looms are introduced in French factories.

1820s: Spinning mills begin operation in Sweden.

Steam power is first used in Czech industry.

1827: A water-driven turbine is invented in France.

1794: The 66-mile Philadelphia and Lancaster turnpike begins operation.

Along an American Highway

1802: In England Richard Trevithick builds his first steam locomotive.

1807: Robert Fulton launches the Clermont, the first commercially successful steamboat, on the Hudson River in New York.

1811: Robert Fulton and his partner launch the first steamboat on the Mississippi River.

Construction begins on the Cumberland Road (later renamed the National Road) from Baltimore, Maryland, to Wheeling, Virginia.

1815: In England John McAdam develops an improved technique for surfacing roads.

1819: The first steamship crosses the Atlantic Ocean.

1825: The 363-mile Erie Canal is completed in America.

In England the first passenger railroad, the Stockton and Darlington Railway, begins operation.

1826: The 2-mile horse-drawn Granite Railroad in Massachusetts becomes the first American railroad.

1790: First American patent law passed.

Philadelphia begins building a public water system.

1798: Robert Owen takes over the New Lanark mills and begins implementing his progressive ideas.

1800: Parliament prohibits most labor union activity.

1802: Parliament passes a law limiting the working hours of poor children and orphans.

1811–1816: Luddite rioters destroy textile machinery in England.

1819: Parliament extends legal protection to all child laborers.

British cavalry fire at demonstrators demanding voting reform in Manchester, killing 11 and wounding hundreds, including women and children.

1827: Carpenters organize the first national trade union in Britain.

18th–century carpenter

1799: Napoleon Bonaparte seizes control of France's government.

1792–1815: The Napoleonic Wars involve most of Europe, Great Britain, and Russia. France occupies many of its neighboring nations, reorganizes their governments, and changes their borders.

1812–1815: War between the United States and Great Britain disrupts America's foreign trade and spurs the development of American industry.

A DATELINE OF MAJOR EVENTS DURING THE INDUSTRIAL REVOLUTION

	1830	1840	1850	1860
REVOLUTIONS IN INDUSTRY AND TECHNOLOGY	1830: Switzerland's first weaving mill established. 1831: British researcher Michael Faraday builds an electric generator. American inventor Cyrus McCormick builds a horse-drawn mechanical reaper. 1834: Bulgaria's first textile factory is built. 1835: Samuel Colt (U.S)invents the Colt revolver. The first steam engine is used to power a paper mill in Croatia. 1836: The first Hungarian steam mill, the Pest Rolling Mill company, begins using steam power to process grain. 1837: The first successful coke-fired blast furnace in the United States begins operation.	American blacksmith John Deere introduces the first steel plow. 1842: Britain lifts restrictions on exporting textile machinery.  Making Bessemer steel	1849: The California Gold Rush begins. 1850: Swedish sawmills begin using steam power. 1851: The Great Exhibition opens at the Crystal Palace in London. William Kelly of Kentucky invents a process for converting pig iron to steel. 1852: Hydraulic mining is introduced in the American West. 1853: The first cotton-spinning mill opens in India. 1856: William Perkin (England) synthesizes the first coal tar dye. Henry Bessemer (England) announces his process for converting pig iron to steel. Isaac Singer (U.S.) introduces the sewing machine.	1859: Edwin Drake successfully drills for oil in Pennsylvania. 1863: Ernest Solvay of Belgium begins working on a process to recover ammonia from soda ash in order to produce bleaching powder. 1864: Switzerland's first major chemical company is established. The Siemens-Martin open-hearth steelmaking process is perfected in France. 1865: The first oil pipeline opens in America. The rotary web press is invented in America, permitting printing on both sides of the paper. 1866: U.S. government surveyors discover the largest-known deposit of iron ore in the world in the Mesabi Range of northern Minnesota.
REVOLUTIONS IN TRANSPORTATION AND COMMUNICATION	1830: The first locomotive-powered railroad to offer regular service begins operating in South Carolina. The opening of the Liverpool and Manchester Railway marks the beginning of the British railroad boom. 1833: The 60-mile Camden and Amboy Railroad of New Jersey is completed. 1835: Construction begins on Germany's first railroad.	1836: First railroad built in Russia. 1843: Tunnel completed under the Thames River, London, England, the world's first to be bored through soft clay under a riverbed. 1844: Samuel Morse (U.S.) sends the first message via his invention, the telegraph. The nation's first steam-powered sawmill begins operation on the West Coast.	1846: First railroad built in Hungary. 1853: The first railway is completed in India. 1854: Americans complete the Moscow-St. Petersburg railroad line. 1855: Switzerland's first railroad opens.	1859: In France Etienne Lenoir invents an internal combustion engine. 1860–1861: The Pony Express, a system of relay riders, carries mail to and from America's West Coast. 1866: The transatlantic telegraph cable is completed. Congress authorizes construction of a transcontinental telegraph line. 1869: The tracks of two railroad companies meet at Promontory, Utah, to complete America's first transcontinental railroad
SOCIAL REVOLUTIONS	1833: Parliament passes the Factory Act to protect children working in textile factories. 1836–1842: The English Chartist movement demands Parliamentary reform, but its petitions are rejected by Parliament. 1838: The U.S. Congress passes a law regulating steamboat boiler safety, the first attempt by the federal government to regulate private behavior in the interest of public safety.	1842: Parliament bans the employment of children and women underground in mines. 1845: Russia bans strikes. 1847: A new British Factory Act limits working hours to 10 hours a day or 58 hours a week for children aged 13 to 18 and for women. 1848: Marx and Engels coauthor the Communist Manifesto.	1854: In England Charles Dickens publishes Hard Times, a novel based on his childhood as a factory worker. 1857: Brooklyn, New York, builds a city wastewater system.	1860–1910: More than 20 million Europeans emigrate to the United States. 1866: National Labor Union forms in the United States. 1869: Knights of Labor forms in the United States. Founding of the Great Atlantic and Pacific Tea Company (A&P) in the U.S.
INTERNATIONAL RELATIONS	1839–1842: Great Britain defeats China in a war and forces it to open several ports to trade.	1847: Austro-Hungary occupies Italy. 1848: Failed revolutions take place in France, Germany, and Austro-Hungary. Serfdom ends in Austro-Hungary.	1853: The American naval officer Commodore Matthew Perry arrives in Japan. 1853–1856: France, Britain, and Turkey defeat Russia in the Crimean War. 1858: Great Britain takes control of India, retaining it until 1947.	1861–1865: The American Civil War brings about the end of slavery in the United States and disrupts raw cotton supplies for U.S. and foreign cotton mills. 1867: Britain gains control of parts of Malaysia. Malaysia is a British colony from 1890 to 1957.

1870	1880	1890	1900

1860s: Agricultural machinery introduced in Hungary.

1870: John D. Rockefeller establishes the Standard Oil Company (U.S.).

1873: The Bethlehem Steel Company begins operation in Pennsylvania.

1875: The first modern iron and steel works opens in India.

Investment in the Japan's cotton industry booms.

1876: Philadelphia hosts the Centennial Exposition.

1877: Hungary installs its first electrical system.

1879: Charles Brush builds the nation's first arc-lighting system in San Francisco.

Thomas Edison (U.S.) develops the first practical incandescent light bulb.

1870s: Japan introduces mechanical silk-reeling.

1882: In New York City the Edison Electric Illuminating Company begins operating the world's first centralized electrical generating station.

1884: The U.S. Circuit Court bans hydraulic mining.

George Westinghouse (U.S.) founds Westinghouse Electric Company.

English engineer Charles Parsons develops a steam turbine.

1885: The introduction of band saws makes American lumbering more efficient.

German inventor Carl Benz builds a self-propelled vehicle powered by a single cylinder gas engine with electric ignition.

1887: An English power plant is the first to use steam turbines to generate electricity.

1888: Nikola Tesla (U.S.) invents an

alternating current electric motor.

1894: An American cotton mill becomes the first factory ever built to rely entirely on electric power.

1895: George Westinghouse builds the world's first generating plant designed to transmit power over longer distances—a hydroelectric plant at Niagara Falls to

Power generators at Edison Electric

transmit alternating current some 20 miles to consumers in Buffalo, New York.

1901: The United States Steel Corporation is formed by a merger of several American companies.

Japan opens its first major iron and steel works.

1929: The U.S.S.R. begins implementing its first Five-Year Plan, which places nationwide industrial development under central government control.

1875: Japan builds its first railway.

1876: In the U.S. Alexander Graham Bell invents the telephone.

German inventor Nikolaus Otto produces a practical gasoline engine.

1870s: Sweden's railroad boom.

1883: Brooklyn Bridge completed.

1885: Germans Gottlieb Daimler and Wilhelm Maybach build the world's first motorcycle.

1886: Daimler and Maybach invent the carburetor, the device that efficiently mixes fuel and air in internal combustion engines

1888: The first electric urban streetcar system begins operation in Richmond, Virginia.

1893: American brothers Charles and J. Frank Duryea build a working gasoline-powered automobile.

1896: Henry Ford builds a demonstration car powered by an internal combustion engine.

1896–1904: Russia builds the Manchurian railway in China.

1903: Henry Ford establishes Ford Motor Company.

1904: New York City subway system opens.

Trans-Siberian Railroad completed.

1908: William Durant, maker of horse-drawn carriages, forms the General Motors Company.

1909: Ford introduces the Model T automobile.

1870: Parliament passes a law to provide free schooling for poor children.

1872: France bans the International Working Men's Association.

1874: France applies its child labor laws to all industrial establishments and provides for inspectors to enforce the laws.

1877: Wage cuts set off the Great Railroad Strike in West Virginia, and the strike spreads across the country. Federal troops kill 35 strikers.

1880: Parliament makes school attendance compulsory for children between the ages of 5 and 10.

1881: India passes a factory law limiting child employment.

1884: Germany passes a law requiring employers to provide insurance against workplace accidents.

1886: American Federation of Labor forms.

1887: U.S. Interstate Commerce Act passed to regulate railroad freight charges.

1890: The U.S. government outlaws monopolies with passage of the Sherman Antitrust Act.

1892: Workers strike at Carnegie Steel in Homestead, Pennsylvania, in response to wage cuts. An armed confrontation results in 12 deaths.

1894: The Pullman strike, called in response to wage cuts, halts American railroad traffic. A confrontation with 2,000 federal troops kills 12 strikers in Chicago.

1900: Japan passes a law to limit union activity.

1902: The United Mine Workers calls a nationwide strike against coal mines, demanding eight-hour workdays and higher wages.

1903: Socialists organize the Russian Social Democratic Workers Party.

1931: Japan passes a law to limit working hours for women and children in textile factories.

1870: The city-states of Italy unify to form one nation.

1871: Parisians declare self-government in the city but are defeated by government forces.

Prussia and the other German states unify to form the German Empire.

1877–1878: War between Russia and Turkey. Bulgaria gains independence from Turkey.

1900–1901: A popular uprising supported by the Chinese government seeks to eject all foreigners from China.

1917: Russian Revolution

1929: A worldwide economic depression begins.

GLOSSARY

AMERICAN SYSTEM: the name British visitors gave the newly devised system of manufacturing that allowed mass production of goods by use of special-purpose machines operated by unskilled workers and involving a strict division of labor

ARISTOCRAT: person born into the upper class of society

ARMORY PRACTICE: what Americans called the "American system" of manufacture, because it was first applied to the production of guns at armories

BELLOWS: a hand-operated pumping device that makes a fire burn hotter by blowing a stream of air on it

BLACKSMITH: worker who uses a hammer and anvil to shape heated iron into objects such as horseshoes

BLAST FURNACE: a tall furnace that uses a blast of air to generate intense heat capable of melting iron and processing it into a purer form

BOYCOTT: an agreement to refuse to buy from or sell to certain businesses

CAPITAL: money or property used in operating a business

CAPITALIST: a person who invests money in a business

CARDING: combing the tangles out of fibers, such as wool or cotton fibers, so they can be spun into thread

CHARCOAL: a fuel made by charring wood in a buried fire so that very little air enters the fire

COKE: a form of coal that has been heated up to remove gases so that it burns with great heat and little smoke

COTTAGE INDUSTRY: manufacturing goods at home

COTTON GIN: a mechanical device that efficiently removes seeds from cotton fibers

DRAWING: a step—between carding and spinning—in the process of turning fibers into thread in which fibers are drawn into a loose strand

DUTY: a tax collected on goods brought into a country

ELITE: a highly select or chosen group of people considered to have high status because of their birth, wealth, education, or social class

EMBARGO: a wartime measure to restrict trade in certain goods or prohibit all movement by trading ships

FORGE: a site where iron is heated in a fire and shaped by hammering

FOUNDRY: a site for melting metal and pouring it into molds to shape it into objects

FULLING: the process of finishing cloth, shrinking and thickening it by wetting, heating, and beating

GAUGE: instrument for judging the precision and quality of a manufactured product

GUILD: medieval form of trade association, whereby men in the same craft or trade organized to protect their business interests

IRONMASTER: one who manufactures iron

JIG: a pattern piece, usually of metal, used as a guide for shaping and duplicating an object with a power tool

LATHE: a machine for shaping pieces of wood or metal, which works by rapidly turning the material against a stationary cutting edge

MACHINE SHOP: a workshop where machines are made or repaired

MACHINE TOOLS: power tools used to make machines or parts of machines

MASS PRODUCTION: production of a large number of identical goods

MERCANTILE: related to trade and the buying or selling of goods

MILL: building with repetitive, rotary machinery for processing an item such as grain, gunpowder, lumber, metal, or textiles. The earliest mills were water-powered gristmills that used millstones to grind grain into flour.

MILLING MACHINE: a machine for cutting or grinding metal

MILLWRIGHT: one who builds or repairs mill machinery

MULE: machine for spinning cotton into thread

PATENT: legal document granting the exclusive right to produce and profit from an invention; the act of obtaining a patent

PIG IRON: the product created by smelting iron ore in a furnace

ROLLING MILL: a mill that uses heavy rollers to form molten iron or steel into sheets or rails

ROVING: twisting textile fibers before spinning them into thread

SMELTING: melting metal ore to extract the pure metal

STATE-OF-THE-ART: most modern version

STEAM ENGINE: an engine that uses steam under pressure to produce power. In the most basic form of steam engine steam enters a cylinder and is then compressed with a piston.

SUBSISTENCE: production of just enough to survive

TANNER: one who processes animal hides into leather

TARIFF: tax on imports; duty

TOLERANCE: the amount by which an object can deviate from a standard size or shape

TRIP HAMMER: a heavy hammer powered by a device that trips it into action

WATER FRAME: a water-powered frame for spinning cotton, one of the earliest machines invented for textile manufacture

ADDITIONAL RESOURCES

BOOKS

Dudley, William, ed. *The Industrial Revolution: Opposing Viewpoints*. San Diego, Greenhaven Press, 1997.

Gourley, Catherine. *Good Girl Work: Factories, Sweatshops, and How Women Changed Their Role in the American Workforce*. Brookfield, CT: Millbrook Press, 1999.

Ingpen, Robert, Robert R. Wilkinson, and Philip Wilkinson. *Encyclopedia of Ideas That Changed the World*. New York: Viking, 1993.

Karwatka, Dennis. *Technology's Past: America's Industrial Revolution and the People Who Delivered the Goods*. Ann Arbor, MI: Prakken Publications, 1996.

Macaulay, David. *Mill*. Boston: Houghton Mifflin Co., 1983.

Macaulay, David. *The Way Things Work*. Boston: Houghton Mifflin Co., 1988.

Olson, James S. *Encyclopedia of the Industrial Revolution in America*. Westport, CT: Greenwood Press, 2002.

Rivard, Paul E. *A New Order of Things: How the Textile Industry Transformed New England*. Hanover, NH: University Press of New England, 2002.

WEBSITES

http://www.americaslibrary.gov
Select "Jump Back in Time"

http://www.fordham.edu/halsall/mod/modsbook14.html
Internet Modern History Sourcebook: Industrial Revolution – provides links to excerpts from historical texts

http://www.kidinfo.com/American_History/Industrial_Revolution.html
Links to numerous online reference resources

http://library.uml.edu/clh/
Website of the Center for Lowell History provides links to numerous online sources

http://www.si.edu/lemelson/centerpieces/whole_cloth/
Smithsonian site about the textile industry

http://www.slatermill.org
Website of Slater Mill Historic Site

PICTURE CREDITS